ISBN: 978-0-578-69950-9

First edition: September 2020

The Way Men and Women Think

Dating and Relationships

Table of Contents

Introduction

INTRODUCTION:
THE OPPOSITE SEX'S THOUGHTS

There's a common misconception that men and women think opposite to one another because of their different biological makeups. This is often attributed as one of the root causes to issues in a relationship. John Gray said it best, "Men are from Mars, Women are from Venus." Fortunately, the goal of this book is to provide insight on the way men and women think. When trying to understand the opposite sex, it can be extremely challenging yet rewarding. While discussing a variety of dating and relationship topics, you'll be able to see through the lenses of, both, men and women. As you read, try to draw connections between both perspectives. Each topic's version was written independently, which means that there wasn't any input from the opposite sex. This provides complete unfiltered authenticity from each perspective.

Now, perspectives come in different shapes and sizes, so there may be a perspective on a topic that you don't agree with. Be open to viewpoints that are different than your own. Elon Musk, the CEO of Tesla, had an extremely different vantage point on how cars should be designed. He SHOCKED the automotive industry, and now competitors are scrambling to catch-up. How does that apply to this book? The perspectives in this book are geared to revamp the way you think about the dating process and focus on how the other person feels.

Before you finish reading, you should be more equipped to interpret and understand the way men and women think. If you're reading this with your significant other, take the time to reflect and converse about each of the topics after you read both versions. Then, see if it's applicable to an area of need in your relationship. Relationships are built upon communication, so why not take a step further and delve into each other's thoughts?

Dating

A simple answer– YES! We're drawn to things that are different than what we're accustomed to. It becomes complicated because it's human nature to be afraid of the unknown in life. If we get in a new situation, we're often filled with anxiety or fear because we don't know what's coming next. However, in relationships, we flirt with the unknown because the opportunity to have something **NEW** or **DIFFERENT** is *exciting*. While we're still fearful of the unknown, we go for it because the reward outweighs the risk.

We all want to feel complete. A void presents itself when we consistently surround ourselves with people that are the same as us in every aspect of life. However, it's an asset to have someone that excels in the areas that are our deficiencies. For example, someone that hates driving would love to be in a relationship with someone that loves driving. That sounds like a match made in heaven.

The biggest misconception about the topic of "Do Opposites Attract?" is the **lasting effect** of this attraction. The initial attraction of someone being different than you isn't something to build a relationship on. For example— A lot of people fall for someone that's different and love it initially, but then they try to *change* the person. That will almost NEVER work. No one wants to be forced to change, but they want to be loved for who they are. So why would they want to change?

SOLUTION: First off, accept that you're attracted to people that are different from you. Without contrast, there's no room for growth. Secondly, if you're currently dating someone, write down 3-5 traits that you like or love about your partner that are different than your own personality traits. By doing this, the next time there's an argument between the two of you, you can refer to this list and remind yourself why you're in love with person.

> *"The challenge of finding someone that loves us for our authentic selves is something we all try to conquer."*
> Maurice Cole

Some people say that "opposites attract," but do they attract in every aspect of one's life. The time and time again, people have this ideal notion that men and women will easily fall in love due to the cinemas often exhibiting this in romantic films. Typically, the films go a little something like this: A woman comes across a man that she is *not* into because they have completely opposite characteristics and interests. Nonetheless, they **somehow** fall in love because— HEY, what do you know— "opposites attract." However, does this truly come to fruition?

Here's why most would say no: People are happier when things are easier. Well, what does that really mean? People enjoy those that have things in common with them. If a partner loves to work out, and the other hates working out, an issue may arise. This is due to the fact that they cannot partake in an activity that they both enjoy and eventually that spirals down to becoming more distant. Distance can cause disconnect emotionally, mentally, and even physically— hence, this is why infidelity has become so pertinent in today's society.

So what do you do when you have imminent love for your partner, but do not have much in common with them? Can the relationship be long-lasting and fulfilling? Is there hope for a promising future? Or will it take time and effort to overcome some of the challenges that the opposing characteristics cause? There are two types of couples in the world: (1) the ones that like it easy and (2) the ones that like it difficult. Being in a relationship is a CHOICE. Who you choose to be with is still YOUR choice! If you are constantly unhappy due to how somebody is or what they like to do, then why are you with them if you can't accept them and their differences? We have all done our fair share of relationship-watching. **NOTE:** Similarly to people watching, relationship-watching involves observing behaviors exhibited by those that are in a relationship. It is commonly found that those that were in relationships and partook in activities that they *both* enjoyed typically had long-lasting relationships.

The first thing a guy will notice about a woman is the way she looks. Any man that says anything different is a bold-faced liar. Men can't help it. It's inevitable— Men are visual creatures that are drawn to physical attributes. It could be anything from a beautiful smile to an apple bottom. With that said, that's what draws men in; however, the reason that men choose to stick around may be *quite* different.

Men jokingly say, "The more attractive she is, the crazier she'll be." And you know what they say— There's a little truth in every joke.

Some clarity on what things guys consider 'crazy': **Clinginess, Obsessive, Triple Texting, Stalking, & Invasion of Privacy**

Like women, men definitely have preferences. The goal of almost every man is to find a woman that's the most attractive to them with the best personality traits. Often, men figure out that the more attractive a woman is, there's other variables that come into play. For example, if she's drop-dead gorgeous— she may get a lot of attention from other men. Some guys can't handle that, so they'd rather settle for a 7 (out of 10). These men would rather settle for less, rather than deal with their own insecurities.

Time to get down to the nitty gritty. What personality traits matter enough to offset the way a woman looks? First, her ability to be understanding is vital. Most men have been tasked with being providers, while being goal-driven in life, so it becomes difficult to allocate a substantial amount of time toward a relationship. Women that are able to recognize that and become an unconditional support system are a dime a dozen. Lastly, there's behaviors like unselfishness, kindness, and forgiveness that are sometimes overlooked but extremely vital. Overall, the ratio of looks to personality varies from guy to guy but looks are definitely more important.

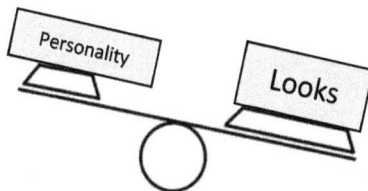

What defines beauty? → Physical appearance or personality ← Many men would say that the way a woman looks matters (A LOT). She has to have the cute face and coke bottle body (or in today's terminology– be "slim thick") in order to peak his interest even a little bit. Heck, some women would even say that they wouldn't give a guy a chance if he didn't have a specific physique, fresh haircut, and clean-cut beard.

Granted, when you first meet somebody— the first thing you see is their external beauty before unveiling their internal beauty. However, some men don't even care about a female's personality because their looks overcompensate for a lack of personality. For example, men often say, "The girl's personality was trash, but she was SOOO bomb," so it didn't matter. He still wanted to talk to her. In this man's case, we could say that 'looks' triumphed.

On the other hand, women love it when a guy is sweet and kind even at the cost of not being physically attractive. Do you know any beautiful women that are dating a man that doesn't equate to their level of attractiveness? Well, the reality is that drop-dead gorgeous girls end-up dating guys that are not the most handsome men (they may even admit), BUT they love them! Why? Women would rather have the guy that is a complete and utter gentleman than a guy that is self-centered, prideful, and arrogant. Most women want the guy that is down-to-earth, shows his vulnerability, and enjoys partaking in intellectual conversation.

Not all men care more about the physicality— you have those rare breeds of men that care about the female's personality more than her physical appearance. Why is this? They realize that physical appearance cannot sustain a relationship. Human beings seek depth, meaning, and fulfillment. If you cannot have thought-provoking conversations with somebody, then how do you expect to grow and build a life with him/her?

"Don't bask in the sweet sensation of the skin when the soul & mind can enrich beyond measure."
Marina Sourial

There's two people, so shouldn't two people pay? Most guys would agree, but they feel some sort of an obligation to pay on the first date. It's definitely a way to show a higher level of interest in the other person. Chivalry isn't completely dead. Guys are taught to show affection through actions. Some examples would include opening doors or placing a jacket over a puddle for a woman to walk over. In today's society, these actions have been a lost art, but they are seen as a sign of a gentleman.

However, why should men pay? Women can't be bought (well, some can, but that's another topic), so why does it matter? Men and women are supposed to build relationships based upon a deeper connection, so money shouldn't have an effect, right? In today's society, both men and women reserve the right to be providers. Women expecting men to pay seems a little outdated, especially since women don't want men to have "expectations" about what will happen at the end of the date if men do end up paying. For example, women don't want to feel obligated to indulge in sexual activities because a man bought them dinner nor should they.

So who pays? Both *can* pay, but men **should** pay. It's an opportunity to show a woman how special she is and that you're capable of providing for her in the future. If a man can't afford to buy a woman a meal, he probably shouldn't be going on dates. Nonetheless, women shouldn't expect a man to pay for them. They should be prepared to pay as well because it's a kind gesture— not a must.

Food for thought: If women don't want to pay for their own meal, why should men?

Most people (women) concur that men should always pay on the first date. It shows that a man is chivalrous, and chivalry is something that most women seek. They want a gentleman— one that will open the car door, pick you up from your house, give you the sweater off of his back, and paying on the first date would fall under this category.

When a man pays for a woman, it shows her that he's interested in her (at the very least). Sometimes, you hear about how *some* males make their date pay half of the bill on the first date. UMMM- awkward. Women take that as: "Am I not cute enough to be paid for?" or "This guy is so cheap!" or "Does he not like me? (Maybe my breath smells?)" Not to mention— If you don't pay for her on the first date, she is probably thinking, "He's definitely never going to take me out and treat me." It's a bad first impression, especially considering that many other men would probably do much more than pay for solely the first date.

If you're a millennial or know a millennial, we have all heard that equality argument. The argument that goes a little something like this: "If men and women are equal, why should men have to pay for women?" It reverts back to the idea of social constructs in society. If you grow up watching your father, grandfather, uncle, etc. pay for everyone at a dinner outing, then that will definitely play a vital role as to what you expect to see in your future boyfriend/spouse. Again, human beings learn certain behaviors due to the environment in which they have been brought up in.

Independent ladies— It's certain you would prefer to pay for yourselves (showing how strong and independent you are that you don't need a man to pay for you). As for the women that seek a gentleman, this is for you– there are still some gentlemen out there.

Don't settle for anything less than what you desire (even if you think he's THAT fine).

The Perfect 1ˢᵗ Date   *Men's Version*

There are sooooooo many variables that go into the perfect first date, but the one that trumps all of them is the person on the date with you. You can be on the beach in Santorini, Greece with an annoying person, so the date ends up being terrible. On the flip slide— you could catch the bus to a local park, and it becomes the most memorable bus ride because of the compatibility with your companion.

With that said— there's a few things to check off for a perfect 1ˢᵗ date: If he says WOW, this can be for 1 of 4 reasons:

1. **The Eye Test**— If a man is mesmerized the 1ˢᵗ time he sees someone, it's considered a WOW moment. He'll never want the night to end and will do whatever it takes to ensure the night goes smoothly.

2. **Good Vibes**— the energy is ultra-important. Without words, the vibe between both people needs to be on the same wavelength. Both people should feel like they're the only two people wherever they go.

3. **Depth**— Now this might be the most important to the trifecta. Nothing is worse on a date then having a connection and thinking someone is attractive, but there's no substance. The personality is the icing on the cake. If a woman shows she can be sweet, make you laugh, and not be crazy– he'll definitely say WOW.

4. **Expectations**— A woman that doesn't have expectations. She doesn't expect a man to pay for her. She's more than willing to pay but appreciates it if he pays for her.

Going 4 for 4 on the above WOW moments leads to a perfect 1ˢᵗ date. Now, if the date is almost over, and he can't check off any of these— he'll say, "wow" but for a completely different reason.

The Perfect 1ˢᵗ Date   *Women's Version*

Lights, Camera, Action!

The man that you have had THE biggest crush on has FINALLY asked you out on a first date. Is it going to be amazing because: (1) it's HIM or (2) you're excited to see what he's going to do for you to show he's really interested? Hmmm ...

Oftentimes, women want to see how a guy is going to treat her to make her feel special. What better way to show her than the first date! RIGHT?! Right. What makes her stand out from the rest of the women in the world that you chose HER to date?

The Blueprint to the Perfect 1ˢᵗ Date:
- ⇒ Picks you up from your house
- ⇒ Opens the door for you as you get into his car
- ⇒ Talks to you in the car about some of your interests (not only his own)
- ⇒ Surprises you by taking you to a restaurant that you've been wanting to go to, and he only figured that out because he did his research in order to tailor the night just for you
- ⇒ Keeps an intriguing conversation at the dinner table
- ⇒ Plans an activity other than just dinner (i.e. bowling, watching the sunset, comedy show)
- ⇒ Drops you off home safely without expectation of sexual activities
- ⇒ Texts you when he gets home about how he enjoyed the night with you

These actions displayed can make a woman feel pretty darn special because (1) it shows his level of interest in you, and (2) it unveils how romantic he is. The perfect first date can sometimes feel like a lot of pressure because both people often want to put their best foot forward. However, it's important to allow your authentic light to shine. It gives your date a better depiction of who you are and what you're really about.

Does *She* Have Goals? *Men's Version*

Yes! She definitely needs goals. Iron sharpens iron. If men are aspiring to be successful individuals, then they need someone with drive beside them day in and day out. Now ... those goals may be slightly different, but they must be present. Men and women should support one another's goals, so each person is held accountable. Deep down, men want to take care of their significant other, but no one wants to help someone that isn't willing to help themselves.

One of the perks of dating a woman that has goals is **time allocation.** Women that have dreams usually have busier schedules. Men love that because they're given an opportunity to (1) miss her and (2) have free time away from her. Absence is sometimes the greatest fuel to a deeper, long-lasting relationship.

Driven men appreciate women with goals much more than women know because they understand the time, effort, and dedication it takes to reach those goals. Also, men are looking to be inspired, too. The weight of the world can sometimes be overwhelming, so it's nice to be able to look over at your partner for a boost of inspiration.

Here are some categories where women have goals that stick out to men: career, fitness, and finances.

Some men love the results of these types of goals but don't understand the ramifications associated with a goal-seeking woman. She may be more successful than her partner. Some men struggle with a 'go-getter' woman because of their own insecurities. The success of one should be the success of the couple, so there shouldn't be any envy. Lastly, the biggest obstacle becomes goal/relationship balance. It's essential for both people to feel valued at the level of the goals. Walking the line between goals and uncompromising companionship is a skill few people master.

> *"If you don't know her goals, how do you know you're both traveling in the same direction?"*
> Maurice Cole

A common thought that runs through a woman's mind is: "Does this guy have aspirations or goals that he would like to achieve in the future?" This says a lot about, not just a man, but *really* any person. It can show how strong-willed, persistent, consistent, and determined he is. All of these qualities are what many women seek. After all, as women, we want to feel a sense of security being in a relationship. Security in the sense of emotional, physical, and financial well-being despite some of the challenges that come our way.

The mere question of: "What are your goals for the future?" can tell you a lot about the person when first dating them. It can give you a sneak peek on what kind of man he is, and if the words he says align with what you want. He may say he has plans to own his own business, doesn't want to have children or to get married, but he wants companionship and wants to travel a lot.

Right off the bat, this tells you A LOT about this guy. 1) He is ambitious and has goals. 2) He does not want to be a father. 3) He is not willing to commit to a life-long relationship. 4) He's adventurous and wants to explore different parts of the world.

If what he wants aligns with what you want, it's likely a good match. Again, more commonalities mean less issues/tension in the relationship. In turn, the relationship will *likely* be more successful.

Now, on the other hand, if some of his responses are deal breakers for you, then you should be very forward and upfront about it from the get-go. You don't need to waste his time, and he definitely does not need to waste yours. False hope is a common trend amongst many men and women.

At the end of the day, a man's goals can show you a lot about what he wants, how you come into play in those goals, and if the both of you are on the same page.

Imagine driving down the street, and a cop pulls you over. They suddenly start going through your car without reason or warning. How would you feel? Would you say something? This is how men feel when women randomly go through their men's phones.

Do men need passcodes? Of course! Every man wants to feel trusted by the woman he loves. Good men are burdened with the consequences of a few bad apples. Infidelities in relationships have led women to second guess their ability to choose a good man. Men simply wanting privacy is a real thing. Imagine if your supervisor/boss (if you have one) micromanaged every decision you made. Would that be a job you enjoyed or an environment conducive for success? Most people would say no. The same thing applies to a relationship. Some men want the opportunity to surprise their significant other with trips, romantic dinners, or spa days, so privacy is an absolute **must**.

Alright alright— There's definitely some red flags that shouldn't be ignored. If all the statements below are **true**, then there's a reason to be concerned:

⇒ Never know where they are
⇒ Never met their family
⇒ Always on their phone and hides it

In this case— sharing passwords should be **mandatory**. Doubt and worry can creep in, and that's unhealthy for a relationship.

Nonetheless— I will say that passcodes may not need to be shared, but making a woman feel secure is definitely necessary. Transparency is key (excluding the surprises mentioned above) to eliminate the fears of the unknown. Simple things like telling them where you're going or who you're with can alleviate some of the trust issues. Women love to feel involved, important, and needed, so let them.

There's nothing better than a woman that trusts her man. With that said— if you're a romantic, keep your password to yourself.

Ladies— is your man on his phone a lot? Does he sometimes smile when he reads something on his phone? Lastly, does he have a password on his phone? To go a step further, have you asked yourself why he has a password on his phone and wonder if he would give it to you?

It can become rather frustrating, overwhelming, and even stressful when passcodes are involved in any relationship. In order to relieve some of this anxiety, communication is extremely vital! It can be a key determinant of a successful or failing relationship. Simply asking him, if you haven't already, "Hey, why do you have a passcode?" can give you more understanding and reduce your anxiety levels. Why? He can tell you directly by answering the question, **OR** he can be deflective and not answer the question. Both scenarios give you loads of insight.

If he responds to your question and says, "I'm just a private person," then that means one of two things: He truly is a private person and does not like people knowing all of his business, **OR** he is saying that just so you do not try to ask to have his password to have access to his "secret world."

If he doesn't respond to the question, it shows that he may be hiding something from you. Nonetheless, it's suspicious behavior! Body language can unveil hints to you as well. If he is hesitant, starts stuttering, shaking, or getting fidgety— these are all indications that should raise a red flag in your head. It shows he is nervous, maybe even scared for you to know what he is hiding. However, you should NOT be afraid to delve into more investigative questions. You need and deserve answers. He needs to provide you with an honest answer, so you have clarity along with peace of mind.

Until then, sneak into his phone when you get the chance. Just kidding … kind of.

Insecurities? Who has them? Just women, right? WRONG! Men have insecurities, too! They just don't vocalize them like women do. Men struggle with insecurities about physical attributes, social statuses, financial statuses, and personality traits. Most people desire to be wanted, so when they're rejected, it affects their self-esteem. Then, men try to overcompensate by taking steroids, buying large cars, or lying about how much money they have to fit a specific mold that society says we need to meet. While struggling with their own insecurities, they downplay the insecurities of women.

A step in the right direction would be communicating these insecurities with women. It's hard for someone to help if they don't know what's going on. It would also help explain some of the illogical behaviors men exhibit. Then, men and women could bond over the insecurities that they both possess.

Men— The secret to dealing with women's insecurities is to simply LISTEN! It may seem silly or unimportant, but if women are willing to be open and talk about it— it matters. The key is reinforcing the things that combat those insecurities. If she struggles with self-doubt about her appearance, tell her she's beautiful in every language possible. If she's dealt with infidelity, make sure she feels secure and remind her she's the only one you want.

Women— Men are tired of dealing with the insecurities caused by past relationships. It's simply unfair to the current guy. If the current guy is the same as the guy's you've dated in the past, why are you dating him? Trust your ability to learn from your past selection mistakes. Give the relationship an opportunity to grow into something you've never experienced.

And if that doesn't work men— just give her your **passcode**.

> *"Life is a dangerous thing. Insecurity is the price of living."*
> Alija Izetbegovic

It's safe to say that almost every woman has experienced a form of insecurity in her life. There may be times where others place unrealistic expectations on women. When women no longer meet those expectations, that's when the deceiving thoughts begin to sneak in. "You're not smart enough, or else you would have made it into that university." "All of these girls on Instagram look perfect. I can't look like that." "Why don't I have a boyfriend? Am I not pretty enough? My personality must be awful." These thoughts can be extremely detrimental to one's self-esteem and mental health.

Your environmental upbringing, social media, those you associate with, and your self-esteem play a part in your insecurities. If your parents called you names regarding your appearance, then you're going to have low self-esteem, which leads to insecurity. If you are constantly looking at edited and photoshopped social media posts, then that isn't going to aid to your insecurity issues either. If your friends are constantly focusing on their image and their presentations, then you may feel the need to keep up to fit the mold. Even if you are the person that is extremely strong-willed and independent, it's a subliminal message to you that you should care about those characteristics as well. After all, you are who you surround yourself with.

Positive affirmation can definitely help with building your self-esteem. Tell yourself that you are beautiful, you are worthy, you are intelligent, you are capable, you are special, and you are loved. When you begin to build the confidence within yourself from YOURSELF, you will start to see a change in behavior. Your insecurities will slowly fade away because you no longer allow others to affect how YOU feel. More power to you, babygirl.

In turn, dating will become quite easy. Why? Because the energy you exude to others is self-love, confidence (which is not to be confused with arrogance), and genuine happiness. It's CONTAGIOUS.

Women often focus on how men change months into a relationship. Let's be real— it's true. Most men have a hard time being vulnerable. No one likes rejection and how much worse would it be if you were putting your true self forward? Human beings, often, put up the façade of one of the following: who we *want* to be or the person we *think* people want us to be. Then if we're rejected, we can detach from the situation a little easier. A great example is when men will be zealous to do absolutely anything in the beginning for their partner, but after six months, that enthusiasm only extends to the things that **he** wants to do. Men get comfortable and start to show their true colors.

Women are not exempted from this behavior either. That's why a lot of women have their hair, makeup, and nails done on every encounter early on. In part— rightfully so. People have been conditioned to have an unrealistic expectation of how our first encounter should be. That leads many to try to imitate a scene in a movie that may have taken 100 different takes, 5 different camera angles, and have scripted lines. Even Leonardo DiCaprio would have issues fulfilling those expectations.

> *"Courage is needed to experience an inexplicably authentic moment."*
> Maurice Cole

Since most put some sort of façade on in the beginning, so how is this overcome? First, being willing to love and accept your significant other if *some* of their behaviors change. People grow and evolve, so the person you met two years ago will be different ten years from now. As long as their core values and love never dwindle, you're in a good place.

Now fellas— want to know if your woman is comfortable around you? Ask her this question— "When was the last time you farted?" If you get an answer, you might be disgusted, but you've moved into a new comfort zone.

Remember the days when you and your boo were just dating? Oh ... no? Don't remember? Too deep into 'The Comfort Zone' that you forgot what it's like to be in the 'lovey dovey' and 'trying to impress each other' stage? It's okay, it's not unusual. It's actually quite common for two people in a relationship to begin feeling extremely comfortable with one another when they have been dating for a long period of time.

Could this be a danger zone though? Quite potentially. With comfort, comes less effort. The person your dating is probably not going to do things that he once did in the beginning of the dating process to constantly impress you. He knows he 'has' you because he has earned and proved himself to you, and he knows that you are invested into him because you have fallen for him.

Naturally, women need (and seek) lots and lots and LOTS of attention. If the man you are dating no longer supplies you with the attention that you want, then you tend to seek it in other ways. Some women might seek the attention from the people on social media, their friends, co-workers, family members, or ... even other men. Not *all* women, but SOME women will resort to looking at other options— even involuntarily. Of course, all women are NOT the same and react differently to certain situations.

If you're a woman that seeks attention and only wants it from your man, you have limited options. First, communicate your concerns to him and give him the opportunity to make the necessary adjustments. If he's not willing to acknowledge your feelings, it may be time for a change.

SIDE NOTE: If the man that loves you does not tend to your concerns or frustrations, does he really love you? Is he really the man that God has intended for you? Just some food for thought.

"Life always begins with one step outside of your comfort zone."
Shannon L. Alder

Calling all men! How do men tell women they GET ON OUR NERVES without telling them they get on our nerves? This sounds like mission impossible. Women have no problem letting men know that something annoys them. Men, on the other hand, are called *controlling* or *impatient* when we express ourselves about what bothers us. Here's an example that every man has experienced:

Remember a time when you were getting ready to go somewhere, and she said, "I'll be ready in 20 minutes." How long did it take? 1 hour and 30 minutes. Ha let's be real, the 20 minutes comment wasn't the only issue. I'm sure you checked on her, and she said, "Almost ready", but that was another 20 minutes. Then, when she was actually finished, she hit you with the, "Are you ready to go?" Uh yeah, I've been ready for the last 2 hours.

Fellas, you want to know how to combat this specific pet peeve (I know there's a ton, but I can only do 1 at a time)— First, hype her up. Let her know she's drop dead gorgeous without any makeup or accessories. This has to be done over and over again before the next date. Next, on the day of the event, tell her the time is 30 to 45 minutes sooner than when it actually is. This won't decrease the time to get ready, but it'll get the process started a lot sooner. Last but not least— pray and hope she takes less time. Haha.

Now, time to cover the most 'common' pet peeve that men experience with women. The indecisiveness of women regarding where or what they want to eat. The biggest lie women say is "I don't care where we eat." Then men pick a million and one places, but it's never good enough. Unfortunately, research has yet to be able to determine a way to EFFECTIVELY solve this specific pet peeve.

Women— you're probably thinking it was never said just to TELL HER. Men already know that does not work, so we can skip that step.

NOBODY IS PERFECT! As much as you'd like to find mister perfect, you may be looking for quite awhile, honey ... and even then, you probably will never find him. Oftentimes, when you start dating somebody, there are certain characteristics that you wished he didn't possess or exhibit. It may be a flat-out flaw or pet peeve of yours. Either way, it bothers you but not enough to keep you from dating him.

Pet peeves can come in the form of social or physical habits. You may not like that when he eats, he always chews with his mouth wide open and very loudly. Or when the two of you go out to dinner, he never uses the handkerchief to put on his lap. If you've used the bathroom after him, maybe you have noticed that he doesn't put the seat down after he's done doing his business.

Maybe, it's not what he does... but what he *says* that absolutely ERKS you? For example: If the two of you are playing basketball, and you beat him. Then, he hits you with the: "You played pretty good... for a woman." UHHH WHAT'S THAT SUPPOSED TO MEAN?! Are women not just as capable as men to play at a proficient or advanced level? It probably never dawned on him that some females have defeated some males in the SAME exact sport.

Whether it be annoying social or physical habits, pet peeves should be addressed to the person that you are dating. It may be uncomfortable because men are sensitive, but you have to voice what bothers you. More often than not, he will be receptive to your concerns and make the necessary changes or improvements, so you're happy. IF NOT— direct him to the door and sing to him: "To the left, to the left... everything you own in a box to the left."

"To the left, to the left"
Beyonce

Every woman wants to be **loved** and **appreciated**. These two things encompass everything a woman wants within a relationship. The desire to love is ingrained within a woman and needs to be replenished by the love of their lives. Most women will never forget the first time they felt true unconditional love from their partner. It could have been as simple as him looking into her eyes as if she's the only one on the planet that exists. Those moments are priceless to women.

It's particularly important for guys to figure their woman's 'love language'. Love is overwhelming and changes everything. Now— the type of love each woman wants is the complicated part. Some women love gestures and physical actions, while some want to feel the love through financial security. Lastly, some women just want you to confess your undeniable love over and over again, so they can hear it. 99.9% of women can agree that a combination of the 3 are a good starting place, but the ways to show love are endless. Here's a few things to do to show your love:

- o Write her a love letter and leave it on her car
- o Cook dinner for her and give her a foot massage during dinner
- o Take her on a shopping spree on a random weekend

Let's not forget women want to be appreciated. A simple *thank you* goes a long way. Women are typically very thoughtful and utilize a lot of time to put those thoughts into action. Men need to acknowledge that and let women know that the details don't go unnoticed. Women want to be a partner and not an object. Women want to be the center of their partner's universe.

Yes— the #1 thing women want includes 2 things. Never simple, but worthwhile.

"To love someone deeply gives you strength. Being loved by someone deeply gives you courage."
Lao Tzu

Women want a man that **listens**.

There will be days where the sun won't be shining. There will be those days where there's overcast, rain and maybe even a little (or BIG) storm. On these days, we need that special guy to simply *listen* to us and put our minds at ease as we vent, eat chocolate, and weep.

A man that has patience to listen to you even with your hormonal imbalances every month is a keeper. Why? Because that shows he genuinely cares about you and your feelings (despite them fluctuating like the weather haha). Let's be real— It's not easy to deal with us when one moment we are crying for no apparent reason and the next, we're clingy-- needing loads of attention.

When a man loves you, he will listen to you. He will pay attention to what bothers you and make sure that he doesn't display the actions that would frustrate you. He will go above and beyond to make sure that you could trust him enough to confide in him— that anything you tell him is safe and sound with him. <u>He will exceed the bare minimum of what is expected of him.</u>

All of these admirable characteristics show you the kind of man he is. If he's showing you that your mental well-being is more important than any kind of physical intimacy, then that is something to be forever treasured because it's— sad to say— rare nowadays.

If a man actively listens to you, he is capable of fulfilling all of your other needs and desires. It ends up being a great addition to improve the overall relationship.

The #1 thing a man wants is to be successful, especially with women. Now, success can be quantified in a lot of ways, but let's simplify it. Men try to avoid the feeling of failing or being rejected because it's a vulnerable state. It's demoralizing, and it's not something you want to feel over and over, again. On the flip side, most men can relate to successfully obtaining the phone number or social media of a woman they find undeniably stunning. That rush of excitement is unmatched.

Men thrive on that success, and it drives the male ego. Women have a monumental impact on the happiness of men. Can you imagine a man in the middle of a marriage proposal, and she says no? The disappointment would be astronomical. The male would be unsuccessful on so many levels: developing a deep enough love connection, deciphering how she feels, and the actual proposal.

Success is KEY. Men, too often, depend on women for that validation— career choices, clothing, living regions, and among other things in some shape or form. What's the point of having a mansion, but you're in it alone? There isn't one, so men strive to successfully satisfy women in every way possible. So how can women help provide this? Verbally reinforce your partner's successful movements, no matter how small. Acknowledging those moments goes a long way. Don't believe it? Let a man give a woman a gift, and she screams "I LOVE IT!" and even gives him a huge hug. Watch his reaction— He'll have a smirk on his face because his gift was a success. Despite what society says, everything with a man is mental, not physical. Anything a man could ever want is connected to success. The top areas where men want to be successful within a relationship: her happiness, seduction, and unconditional love.

With all that said— in those petty arguments, let him win. Yes, you read correctly. It'll bring back that feeling he had when the both of you first met. It's shocking, but true.

Men want a woman that sets herself apart from the rest.

What does that entail?
1. Physically Attractive
2. Ambitious
3. Independent

These are some of the characteristics that men are subconsciously paying attention to. If a woman embodies these characteristics, then a man feels that she can add value to his life.

If a woman is absolutely stunning, a man, subconsciously, is already thinking about how attractive she is and how that can play a role in their sexual encounters. Not to mention, a woman with jaw-dropping looks can be his arm candy. Men want to feel proud of who they are with, and it aids to their ego if other men are envious.

If she is ambitious and goal-oriented, a man can easily be drawn because it shows that she is driven, hard-working, and does not confine herself to limitations. This is attractive to a man because not all women possess these characteristics. It is difficult to come by. The road less traveled on is usually the road that is more difficult and **THAT** is much more appealing from outsiders looking in.

When a woman is independent, a man becomes intrigued because he sees how common it is for many women to be dependent on others, especially a man. So, if he finds a girl that is self-reliant and has respect for herself, then that is something that is treasured and appreciated. It shows that she does not NEED anybody, but she merely WANTS somebody.

Long-term, these are key characteristics that incline a man to date a woman because he envisions a potentially great life partner, best friend, and/or wife.

Relationships

Why do women always assume that men think they're *crazy*? Uh … because it's kind of true. Men have formulated an opinion about women through stories passed down from generation to generation. Almost every man has heard this phrase, "You think I'm crazy? I'll show you crazy." What non-crazy person says this? Ask a man, and he'll say nobody. Ask a woman, and she'll say a woman in love that's been in love and hurt. But is there really a difference between being crazy and being in love?

Loving someone more than yourself can be viewed in itself as being crazy. It goes against one of the 1st aspects of human nature: self-survival. However, it's an element of *crazy* that each human being should strive to feel and exemplify. Women are the absolute best at this. They dive headfirst into the pool of love, and it's sometimes hard to control some of the emotions associated with love. Men are, sometimes, surprised by how fast and strong women feel. For example, a woman has been dating a man for two weeks, and she's head over heels for him. She tells him, "I love you, and I want to have your kids!". Some men, frankly most, are freaked-out by this comment. Men can't comprehend how the feeling of love could grow in such a short span of time. Timing is everything. If that same comment was said after a year of being in a relationship, it would have a different impact.

Furthermore, there's other areas that men misinterpret as *crazy*, and they're usually tied to **insecurities**. Most of the time, women aren't the culprit of the root cause of these insecurities. Usually, it's connected to something that has occurred in the past, a void their partner isn't filling, or a psychological impact from social constructs. These insecurities can lead to women:

⇒ Going through your phone without your permission
⇒ Driving by your place to make sure you're alone
⇒ Counting dishes to make sure no one has been there

Yes, these behaviors aren't okay and are a little *crazy*. However, it's a man's responsibility to create a level of security that a woman doesn't feel a need to exhibit any of these behaviors. Communication is key to overcome these obstacles. Women are fragile and priceless, so they need to be treated as such.

So yes— a woman in love is ~~sometimes~~ usually crazy. If you're a man, and you want a woman to fall in love with you ... aren't you the crazy one?

FROM

TO

Have you ever been called 'crazy' by a man that you once dated or even by the man you're currently dating? It's an adjective that men like to carelessly use to describe a woman's behavior when she reacts to a man's actions. Another case of this term being thrown around is when a man notices that his woman becomes possessive of him, wants to spend lots of time with him, or simply needs attention from him.

Granted, when women exhibit questionable action, it yields for probable cause to call a woman 'crazy.' For instance, a woman slashing her man's tires because he cheated on her. This is NOT okay, under any circumstances. It's quite simple— simply leave the relationship. When women start acting out of character, then the term 'crazy' may be warranted (but even then, there are better words that could be used to describe her).

Needless to say, men really need to constantly stop calling women, 'crazy'! It's getting old, it's provoking, and it isn't healthy to hear repeatedly (especially if not warranted)! Any woman can concur that the healthier and more effective way of handling situations with your woman is actually talking to her about what bothers you and giving her positive affirmation— saying "Honey, I know you exhibit certain behaviors to show the depth of your love for me."

That's really what it comes down to— love. If a woman does not care about a man's actions and does not check on you from time to time, does she really love you? Does she really care and value the relationship that you guys have? What a man thinks is 'crazy' is misunderstood for a woman being extremely in love with her man. The day that men come to this realization will be the day that both parties in the relationship will be happy.

"Love recognizes no barriers. It jumps hurdles, leaps fences, penetrates walls to arrive at its destination full of hope."
Maya Angelou

The other side of the comfort coin. To be engaged in a serious relationship, men and women **must** be able to communicate their innermost thoughts. Women are known to be a little more open and are willing to discuss their deepest darkest fears with their girlfriends. Men, on the other hand, will bottle those thoughts and only talk with their guy friends about surface level issues. It's not common that a man will go to another man and express how he feels like he's failing at life. But when a man has a woman that makes him feel like he has a safe haven, he's willing to share that kind of information with her. Men LOVE having a woman that they can confide in and be their true selves with.

IMPERFECTIONS / **COMFORTABILITY**

With that said— women need this comfort zone as well! Women deal with insecurities that some men can't even begin to comprehend. The social constructs in society have ingrained unrealistic expectations for the queens in the world— from body sizes, skin complexions, and nonexistent imperfections. Women's imperfections make them beautiful, and men should fully want to embrace that. The sooner women feel loved, despite the clothes they wear or the shade of mascara, the sooner those social constructs can be broken. The best part of a relationship is having someone else to lean on in tough times. The key is being vulnerable enough to trust your partner with your inner most thoughts, while being understanding when they fall short in comforting you. Most people in relationships aren't sociologists or therapists, so they're responses may not be exactly what you want to hear. But you know what … they're trying to be there for you and that's what counts.

"True love turns imperfections into perfection."
Maurice Cole

Have you reached that anticipated part in the dating process where you and your significant other feel comfortable confiding in one another? This can be quite exciting and a little nerve-wracking because a lot of vulnerability lies within this part of a relationship.

It takes a lot of courage, trust, and strength to be completely vulnerable and, ultimately, comfortable with somebody.

There are a few factors to consider:
(1) What does your significant other's relationship background look like? Did he have any issues in his past relationships, or was he cheated on? If he did have a past where his trust was lost, you might need to be patient with him because he may be still scarred from his previous relationship. His vulnerability guard is likely to be SKY HIGH. Again, it will take patience and time to prove that he can trust you.

(2) Have you observed how he responds to those with opposing viewpoints to his? Is he courteous and respectful of other people's opinions, or is he rude and disrespectful? If he is courteous and respectful of others' opinions, you've got yourself a winner! Why? You must remember—that you may not agree with him on everything, so how he treats other people is likely how he will treat you.

(3) Is he trustworthy? Does he keep information to himself, or is he loose-tongued? If he has proved that he is trustworthy through his actions, then you will be more inclined to share information with him because you know that your business won't be spreading like wildfire. TRUST IS KEY TO ANY RELATIONSHIP.

TRUST · STRENGTH

COURAGE

"Life begins at the end of your comfort zone."
Neale Walsh

Is PMS'n an Excuse?   *Men's Version*

Every woman on the planet has experienced, "That Time of the Month." Men are silly enough to argue with women about this. There's very little, if anything, that a man can say to win an argument during this period. Women, on the other hand, feel a sense of extreme freedom during this time period. A majority of women believe that anything they do wrong is covered under the **Menstrual Period Act** established in 1403 B.C. Men have failed, time and time again, to prove this theory wrong. Here's a man's opinion:

First and foremost, the menstrual cycle period is something that is undeniable. Women go through excruciating pain, blood loss, and hormonal changes. Men should be compassionate and provide assistance during these tough times. Month over month, men should be able to become experts at being a great support system. With that said, month over month, women should get better at coping with PMS'n. Empathy is definitely required, but all behaviors caused by PMS'n shouldn't be excused. Accountability is important in every relationship and that includes when we're going through a tough situation.

If you disagree and feel like women shouldn't be accountable for any of their actions while PMS'n … answer the following 2 questions:

1. A marine suffering from post-traumatic stress disorder shoots someone while having an episode. Is PTSD a valid excuse?
2. A male with high testosterone cheats on his spouse. Is the high testosterone a valid excuse?

If your answer was "No" to either, how could PMS'n possibly be an excuse for any inappropriate behavior?

> *"We aren't defined by what happens to us in life, but by how we react and evolve from those events."*
> Maurice Cole

Is PMS'n an Excuse? *Women's Version*

So it's that time of the month. It's the first day— the cramps are kickin', the blood is flowin', the hormones are ragin', **AND** the chocolate is callin'.

During this time, the people around you (whether it be your family, boyfriend, co-workers, or friends) know when you're PMS'n. Though women become very moody, women also become extremely *needy*. This truly sucks for the boyfriends (God bless their precious souls). Why, you may ask? Well, when women run out of pain medication, who must they ask to run to Target for them? That's right, boo-thang. Oh, but what if the meds aren't effective enough to relieve the pain that they're experiencing? Some women have to resort to heating pads, personal hand massages from their significant other, and/or some hot chamomile tea with honey. All of this merely aides to the physical pain women experience.

What about the hormonal imbalances? How do boyfriends tend to that? Well, chocolate, ice cream, junk food— pretty much anything unhealthy— does the trick. If women's sporadic cravings are satisfied, then women tend to be a little happier, even if the end result means gaining 10 pounds in one sitting.

The hassle that men go through in order to make women feel better can sometimes take a toll on them. This is understandable. However, some men begin to think that some women use the PMS as an excuse for the man to do everything for her. UH WRONG! What women go through is beyond REAL! Why would anybody fake that? Clearly, there are some women out there that *might* fake a little pain for some extra attention, but a few bad apples don't represent all women.

PMS IS REAL— not an excuse by any means. Men, the moral of the story is ... next time you see your lady cramping, do yourself a favor and buy her some chocolate.

Ex-es play a vital role in our lives. They contributed to happy memories, and they were likely once a particularly good friend. With that said, you *can* be friends with your ex-, but you probably shouldn't. Here's why:

When you're in a relationship, one of the main goals is to make your partner feel secure. They shouldn't have to worry about any of your past relationships interfering with the current relationship. At one point in time, you fell in love with your ex-, so your partner is always going to see that person as some sort of threat. If it's hard to give up that friendship, then an important question to ask is— "Why do I need to be friends with them?" In relationships, people already sacrifice spending time with friends with people that they haven't dated (well they should). Why should ex-es be any different?

There are some situations that are exceptions. One example is if your partner has kids with an ex-. The well-being and security of the kids trumps any relationship. If this situation presents itself, clear guidelines need to be set within the relationship so both parties are comfortable. Trusting your partner is vital, so if you're having trust issues— SAY SOMETHING. How you feel needs to be out in the open, so the issue can be resolved. A way to ease some of the trust issues would include:

⇒ limiting communication with ex-es to only things related to the kids
   or
⇒ Both, your partner and you, always interacting with the ex-

The latter suggestion allows you to always be aware of any interaction that occurs but requires you to be respectful to their ex- and see them often. A good way to help you interact graciously is to remind yourself that their ex is someone that helped mold your partner into who they are today. Also, their mistakes are the reason you have the opportunity to date your partner.

So yes— being friends with ex-es is perfectly fine but avoid it if you can.

Can Ex-es Be Friends? *Women's Version*

A person that you previously dated needs to remain a person of the past.

It is *not* wise for you to remain in contact with somebody that you are no longer with. Ties were cut off for a purpose. Sometimes, it's difficult because you may feel like you've invested so much of your time into that person, you have had so many fond memories that you created together, or that person was simply your best friend. However, it is not emotionally healthy to cling to people that are no longer with you in the present.

If you remain friends with your ex-, and you're dating somebody new, how do you think your current partner would feel about that? That can definitely be problematic in a newly established relationship. Don't you think there is a chance that feelings could linger for your ex- since you are still in contact? Or that you might get back together? It's likely that you can become vulnerable and start making emotionally based decisions, which may result in going back to the same cycle of being with a person that truly is *not* for you. It just seems like a recipe for disaster!

Now, please think about— how would remaining friends with your ex-aide to your current relationship? There is going to be a lot of insecurity, skepticism, and uneasiness in the midst of the relationship. If it's not helping your relationship, it's harming it.

Ex-es aren't friends. They're ex-es. Don't do a disservice to yourself or your current/future significant other. Both, you and your significant other, deserve a healthy relationship.

> *"An 'ex' is called an 'ex' because it's an **EX**ample of what you shouldn't have again in the future."*
> Unknown

Space might be the key to any successful relationship. Men are unique creatures that need the opportunity to miss their significant other. The saying, "You don't fully appreciate things until they're gone" holds true most of the time. Hence why time apart gives both people a chance to miss one another. When people are able to take a step back from life, they're able to view things in a new light. The little annoyances don't seem as bad, and the good memories start to fill the empty void.

Oftentimes, women mistake men wanting "space" as a lack of love in the relationship. This couldn't be further from the truth. Men need the ability to make **choices**. If he has the option to hang out with his friends or you, and he chooses you, he's more likely to enjoy the time spent with you. Think back to your childhood when you were forced by your parents to eat vegetables. Did they taste amazing? Probably not, because the decision wasn't yours. Men are the same way when it comes to hanging out with women. That's why 90% of men enjoy time spent early on in relationships, rather than after years into one.

No one wants to feel like they've lost themselves, and sometimes too much time together does that. It's healthy to have time for friends or hobbies that helped mold you into the person they fell in love with. Sometimes it's hard because one person may be clingy, but there's a solution ... the first moment you have after some "space", show an unequivocal amount of appreciative emotion towards your lover, and they'll remember why they love you so much. They'll forget about the space and focus on the moment right in front of them. Then ... you can plan your next time for space.

Disclaimer: Extra space was left at the bottom of this page for men desperately seeking some from their partner. Have fun.

In the process of building a relationship, space is a CRUCIAL component. Early on, expectations of time need to be managed, so there's a solid foundation.

Stage 1: "I Think You're Cute"
Ladies— It's known that all women love a confident man. Somebody that isn't afraid to show his masculinity nor his vulnerability. Women also like a man that does not come off as a creep. So guys— how do you show you're interested in a woman without being a complete creep? Well, this is where space comes into play. Of course, other factors play a role such as personality, approach, appearance, body language, and overall demeanor, but space— SPACE is vital! It could make it or break it. For example: If a guy was trying to talk to a woman that he sees at the gym every day and drops compliments here and there, then she probably wouldn't feel creeped-out (probably just flattered). On the other hand, if the guy is pestering her everyday with endless compliments, then she MIGHT start thinking he's obsessive, or he's a pervert. Bottom line— space and moderation can help you get to the next step in the relationship process. NEXT.

Stage 2: "We're Talking"
So he made it passed "Stage 1," and you gave him your number. The both of you start chatting it up over the phone and texts. In this stage, it is vital that you keep distance because either person can lose interest rather quickly. Here's why— smothering or clinginess can scare someone away ... The alert that goes off in their head says— "RUN!" At this stage, learn about the person, if you start to form a connection and begin developing feelings, try to resist overly expressing them. If this stage is passed successfully, that will lead you to Stage 3!

Stage 3: "In A Relationship"
Ladies, we got him now. You got the title, so space goes out the window. Have fun!

Yes! All men know that their mom must approve. There's a marriage study that examined the accuracy of the mother's opinion about failed relationships. In 10 out of 10 cases, men claimed their mom disapproved of their past partner. All of the mothers said the same thing, "I told you there was something I didn't like about her!" Alright— that may be facetious, but isn't that how it seems? Mother's always want the best for their kids, so they either have unrealistic expectations for who they date, or they're just protective. Either way— it's a part of the innate nurturing skills that's given to mothers.

With that said— men should totally take advantage of this source of information. They have an irreplaceable perspective because they're women themselves, so they can teach men a thing or two. They may see tendencies that they once exhibited in the past, and they want to protect their kids from those headaches. Unfortunately, men are hard-headed, sometimes. It occasionally takes a first-hand experience of these headaches because a pretty face and coke-bottle shape can definitely be blinding.

Now, there are times where a mother's expectations are unreasonable for the person their child dates. For example— Not dating someone because of their socioeconomic status, or ethnicity. Being able to decipher between personal biases or helpful insight is key when seeking advice. If your mother tells you, "She's only with you for your money." Keep that thought in your mind and investigate for yourself. If you pay for everything, try to split the bill on the next date and see how she treats you. Give your significant other the opportunity to disprove any red flags pointed out from parents.

There are so many benefits to your mother liking who you love. It's like a second pair of eyes on the relationship. If your mom sees you messing up, she'll tell you because she wants to keep *this one* around. You've probably heard the "Be nice to her," and if you haven't … she's not the one.

So say you've been dating this guy for a few months now, but you want to know what your mom thinks of him. You've already told her how cute he is because he has been *nothing* but sweet to you. He seems like an *ideal* guy. Hmmm … but your mom wants to see if it's all for show or if that's how he really is. After all, mama DOES know best …

Here's how it would play out:

One day, you invite him over for dinner with your parents, so they can get to know 'mister perfect.' He shows up with flowers and maybe a bottle of wine. Not to mention, he comes through the door ready to impress— suit and tie, fresh haircut, and luring aroma. Your immediate thoughts are (1) He's fine. (2) Mom is *probably* impressed with what she sees. Then you realize, mama is no fool. These aren't the details that help a mom classify a man as a keeper.

So if these initial indicators aren't what make a difference to mama's opinion, what does? She analyzes him based on his character, his goals, the way he treats you, and the way he treats his mom. Mama's take a holistic approach and aren't blinded by physical attraction, so they can see the tendencies that will hurt you in the long run. Now, does that stop you from dating him? Of course not, because you want to find out for yourself if your emotional investment is stronger than her intuition. It's obviously more convenient to date someone that the family approves of, but there's other factors at hand. Each person, including mamas, have their own personal biases. At the end of the day, you're the person that must wake up next to your partner each and every day, so the decision should be yours. If you can sleep at night peacefully with whatever decision you make, then be happy and do you boo!

Yes! Secrets are necessary from time to time. Women— you might think this is a joke, but it's true. Relationships should be built on trust, love, and respect. With that being said, secrets are essential for any GREAT relationship. Now ... if an average relationship is what you're seeking, then secrets don't need to exist.

Both men and women will be required at one point or another to keep a secret from each other. It takes creativity to fulfill the love women desire. Surprises are a key component of elevating a relationship to the next level. Time to dig a little deeper. The phrase, "Some things are better left unsaid," was created to reference all the secrets you should keep in a relationship. Women love asking questions, but the actual answer to the question isn't always what they want to hear. Here's two questions, with answers they want to hear instead of a direct answer:

Question 1: "Do I look fat in this dress?"
Correct Answer: "You look absolutely stunning! Why would you ask me that?"

Question 2: "Do you think she's cute?"
Correct Answer: "Babe, you're the only one I see!"

Notice, you're communicating the truth and providing reassurance. At the same time, you're technically keeping a secret because you didn't answer the questions. Sometimes, this is best because the goal is to make her happy ... not create an unnecessary fight. Women are complicated, but there's typically some sort of solution to any conversation.

Furthermore, secrets that are connected to ill intentions are **not** okay and can be detrimental to a relationship. Good men and women use secrets to elevate a relationship. Immature individuals with a lack of respect choose to mask their true motives through secrets. Where do you stand?

Are Secrets Healthy? *Women's Version*

Secrets are NOT healthy. It can leave your partner's mind wandering, which can lead to *extreme* insecurities. If communication is the boat to of any relationship, then transparency is the anchor. Women need reassurance time and time again, and secrets only prohibit that. Women want to tell their significant other everything: how their day went, their deepest fears, and their frustrations. They expect the same from their boo. Women are searching for a best friend in a significant other, so they may confide in them and show their vulnerable side (which often comes with comfortability and time).

Secrets cause women to worry and to be insecure. When men say that they are 'private' and do not share much information about themselves or their daily activities, it automatically raises red flags in a woman's mind because it seems that they are hiding something. Men should provide that reassurance and open up more. Transparency can go a long way in the evolution process of a relationship. Women love a man that's not afraid to show his emotions and vulnerability. Society has tried to program men and women into believing that women are weak and incapable of hearing the difficult things men have to say. Well— they're wrong. Women are strong-minded individuals and can handle all secrets. So speak up fellas! The more information the better!

Don't forget— women have secrets too. There are things in the past they want to keep to themselves: the number of men they have dated in the past, how much money they spend on clothes, moments when they need to fart, etc. Just as much as women want answers to their questions, men want answers too. Men have been trained to not show any indications of insecurities to women because it's a sign of weakness, but it doesn't mean that they do not have them as well. So ladies— if men are brave enough to ask certain questions, then they, too, deserve to receive answers and know the truth about matters that may be outside of your comfort zone.

It is all a part of the growth process. With secrets, come insecurity and worry. With vulnerability, come fruitfulness and evolution. Which will you choose?

Silence or Confrontation   *Men's Version*

All men know— there's **NO** right answer to this question. Men and women view problems differently. One sex views it logically, another emotionally. Decipher which group you're in. Nonetheless, below gives an account of how men can conduct themselves in this unwinnable situation.

Ah confrontation! The word itself sounds aggressive and 80% of the time that's how men come off when addressing a problem with their significant other. In theory, it should work. Right? For instance, saying, "Hey, we have a problem. Let's discuss it." This provides an opportunity to acknowledge the problem together. Most would say this is a good thing. Now, if both people agree on the solution for the problem, this route is great, but that isn't always the case. And when there's disagreements— the conversation changes, and it becomes less about the issue itself but about how you conduct yourselves within the fight. Imagine this— your girlfriend comes to you and says "Hey, I don't like her. Can you stop talking to her completely?" Now it's someone you've never dated and have known your entire life. You respond, "I've known her my whole life. We're just friends." She starts crying and says, "You don't care about how this makes me feel." or "You care about her more than me?" What do you do? ... Don't worry there's no right answer besides what she wants. Don't think it's true? Ask her right now.

Now fellas— it seems like the only option left is being silent right? Try being silent when a woman expresses her concerns about an issue. It'll drive her nuts and make her even more mad, and you'll hear "You don't have anything to say? You don't even care about my feelings" Then, they'll start asking and answering questions themselves "Oh so you're just going to stay quiet? Do you even care? I knew you didn't love me." Like what? How did you get that from silence?

Moral of the story— Men neither one works, so just pick your battles wisely. Just say, "I love you, babe. Can we focus on that because I need you in my life?" That'll buy you 5 minutes to decide if it's something worth arguing about.

How do you deal with issues with *mister* dream guy when they arise unexpectedly?

Say things are going great between you and the guy that you are dating. He's been super sweet— opening your door, making sure you walk on the inside of the crosswalk, holds your hand, kisses your forehead, doesn't rush things, etc. Then, you go to dinner, and you see his eyes wandering at dinner (Ladies, you know how that goes). This begins to bother you, but you're not quite sure how to approach the issue. So you begin to contemplate— should you stay quiet, **OR** should you tell him that it bothers you, considering that it could blow up into an even larger issue?

This can be a huge internal conflict for some women, especially considering that you may not know how he will react. It really reverts back to your personality and how you deal with things best for your own sanity and peace of mind. After all, your mental health and state-of-being is most important in this case.

If you internalize your thoughts, feelings, and emotions and that has worked for you in the past because you would rather deal with it and avoid even further conflict, then by all means, do what keeps your mental sanity intact!

Contrary to this, if you are accustomed to expressing yourself and how you feel, regardless of any backlash, then by all means do so! Sometimes, you need to vent, gain clarity, and seek resolution to the issue, so it does NOT happen AGAIN in the future. However, if the two of you cannot come to common ground or to some sort of understanding on each end, you may want to come to acceptance that the two of you are not as perfect for each other than you may have thought. Again, you want to do what works best for YOU!

In life, some things require sacrifice. It's what you are willing to sacrifice! Just remember— never sacrifice your mental well-being for a temporary somebody.

Yes! Of course, the male's version is going to say yes, but do you know why? Now, most people think sex matters because it **feels** good— that's false. That's a result of sex (for most), but that's not why it's important.

Sex matters because it puts blinders on within a relationship. It covers up the negative traits or actions exhibited by a significant other. Hence why a lot of people stay in relationships a lot longer than anticipated with partners they don't have a deep connection with. A relationship without sex allows two people to build the foundation of their relationship. Connections based on personality, compatibility, or common interests show a higher success rate for long-term relationships.

On the positive side, sex is a way to show affection. It's an outward expression of your inner feelings. Love intensifies when the element of touch is incorporated. When you're intimate with someone, you're giving them a piece of yourself, while taking a piece of them. That can be good and bad. It builds a connection that isn't supposed to be broken. Needless to say, this is why sex was reserved for marriage since the beginning of time. There's a reason why men and women are crafted into forms that fit perfectly together, and it's deeper than procreation.

Sex definitely matters, but TIMING is everything. Following the correct blueprint determines whether sex has a positive or negative impact on a relationship. Pre-marital sex causes problems in the long run because partners become unidentifiable. Post-marriage, sex helps a couple overlook the unimportant aspects of the relationship and helps reinforce the love the two shares. It's kind of like going to the store. If you walk out of the store with a bag of chips without paying and start eating, it's a crime. With that same bag of chips, if you pay first then eat and leave— you have a delicious bag of chips (if they're Hot Cheetos).

> *"If marriage is food, then sex is water. After we eat, we all get a little parched."*
> Maurice Cole

SEX. That is why we are all living and breathing. Our parents had to have sex in order for us to be birthed into this world. Besides the reproductive aspect of it, sex can be a beautiful display of affection to express love for a significant other. Does sex matter? Yes.

Sex has been highlighted all over the media, in films and even television shows, to portray various reasons why people partake in the act. For some people, they just want to "hook-up," which means they just want to toot it and boot it with no commitment or "no strings" attached. Most people that are in relationships have sex to show the love that they have towards one another (besides the ones abstaining from sex before marriage— that's another conversation in itself).

Society coined a term to solidify the importance of sex in the world— Virginity. Younger women are somctimes defamed or ridiculed for losing their virginity too soon. While males, on the other hand, are acclaimed by society. Most can agree that sex is important, but the reason why it's important is a different story. Below are 4 reasons why women might find sex important:

1. Purity/Innocence— Waiting until Marriage
2. Intimacy— Physical Connection with Partner
3. Physical Pleasure
4. Completeness— Emotional Connection with Partner

So does sex matter? Yes. However, at what point should it not matter as much? When your relationship begins to become consumed by sex, then the act of affection needs to be re-evaluated. If every time you see your significant other and all you do is have sex, there's room for concern.

All in all, women are searching for intimacy and that's deeper than just sex. Being stimulated mentally and connecting with a man on multiple levels is the ultimate goal. The simple touches like holding hands, back tickles, or long eye gazes give the ultimate climax.

Marriage— Why?　　　　　*Men's Version*

> *"We get married because we love the other person more than anything else in the world and there's nobody else that we want to be with. Since I was a kid, I dreamt of my wedding day and standing next to my soulmate"*

That's what men say when asked why they should get married— sounds good, right? Everyone comes back to reality. Men are ~~different~~ than women. A man that's going to get married <u>should</u> love the person he's marrying more than anybody else (minus Jesus and his kids, but that's a separate conversation). However, that's not **why** men get married. Men get married because that pleases God and makes women happy. Oh, let's not forget— to keep her from everybody else.

A lifetime commitment, expensive wedding, expensive ring, and if the marriage doesn't work— alimony. **YIKES**— that sounds scary. Even so, a man's love and commitment to make their woman happy outweighs all of that. While stepping to the plate, men try to provide what their soulmate has been dreaming of their entire life. It becomes easy when looking at the pros and cons. The one that usually tips the scale is living without the woman you love. Smart women will only stick around *so long* before they start recognizing their worth of something much more. That's typically when guys try to wake up and get their act together.

Okay women— the truth is a hard pill to swallow sometimes, so here's some clarification: Marriage is a blessing. Two people are joined together as one, and you gain a life partner. Lives are built together, and everlasting memories are made each and every day. Most guys are grateful that women want to get married because it shows that the women see a future with them. It just takes time for men to get on the same wavelength. One day, men will realize that marriage makes the relationship a little bit easier. It gives women security because they feel official.

Men, tell your future wives why you ~~really~~ want to get married. If you don't know, refer to the quote above.

Why should somebody get married? To have a lifelong partner that gives you pure, genuine & irreplaceable love. If you had that kind of love, would you want to seek somebody else? Most would say **no**. Why? They don't want to hurt their significant other and/or don't want to tarnish what they already have.

So how do you differentiate between not dating other people and marriage? Society has ingrained into people the concept of getting married because you've been dating for a certain amount of time. That's why in some states there's a common law marriage reserved for those in relationships that have been cohabitating for an extended period of time. Is this really a viable reason to get married?

Aside from the length of time you've dated someone, what else matters? Our upbringing. Human beings learn certain behaviors due to the environment in which they have been brought up in. If somebody grows up in a household where the parents are married and happy, then he/she too are likely to exemplify those practices. You can't forget about how you grew up watching television shows about couples getting married, having the big and elaborate weddings, the men picking out the ostentatious diamond rings and getting down on one knee. OH— and you can't forget about those tax breaks! Haha. Society does a great job of unveiling the unimportant aspects of marriage. Why? Capitalism— to gain profit for one's self.

Marriage is and should be special. Marriage is a once in a lifetime experience (for some anyway). For those of religious belief, marriage is a unity between two people in front of God. It's a way of passage into the sexual realm. Thus, leading to sexual intimacy (a gift that God bestows upon the newly wed). Imagine waiting to have sexual intimacy with somebody that you deeply and undeniably love until the wedding day. That would be special for two reasons: (1) Assuming your significant other waited as well, you both share something that is not shared with anyone else and (2) You're being obedient to God and His Will for your life.

After Thoughts

AFTER THOUGHTS: WHAT NOW?

Since of the beginning of time, men have been trying to figure out what women want (and vice versa). It has been so crucial that they even created a movie about it, "What Women Want." Even in that film, Mel Gibson had to hear the woman's thoughts to truly understand her. Thoughts are unfiltered and a gateway to a person's heart. Actions are important too, but people, sometimes, misinterpret someone's actions because of how society defines them, or a previous bad experience tied to that specific action.

The goal of this book is to transpire intellectual thoughts and reflections upon our interactions with the opposite sex. There is no doubt that men and women have differing views on the things that emerge in life. Perspectives will vary, but the secret here is *understanding*. Understanding where the other person is coming from can go a long way in dating and relationships. It shows a certain level of respect for the other person, and it allows for progression. Areas of your relationship can progress in ways you and your significant other never thought would be imaginable. It is, here, where you can garner a deeper love for each other. Ninon de L'Enclos best explains the dilemma men face when trying to understand women in the quote below:

"A man is given the choice between loving women and understanding them."

Hopefully, the words in this book have given both, men and women, enough information to bridge a gap between loving each other and understanding one another. Time and effort are all it takes to really understand someone's perspective. With that said, **your thoughts** and **opinions matter**. There are two blank pages at the end of the book, so you can express how you felt reading this book or if you have a differing perspective on one of the topics. Send us a photo of what you wrote to our Instagram or email.

Instagram - @thewaymenandwomenthink
Email – mandmwritinggurus@gmail.com

Your Thoughts _____ *Version*

Thank You

1st Corinthians 10:31